evergreen
by
keiran james

cover by ann-sofie vejs

also by keiran james

ephemerality

Copyright 2021

All rights reserved.

the playlist.

an evergreen grows in my backyard.

most of the pieces in this book were written years ago. i kept wanting to save them for a future book, but just like an old friend who has overstayed their welcome, i wanted them gone. it felt cruel to simply erase them, even though they feel juvenile compared to the writer and the person i am now, but they are a part of me. they are me. the words i scribbled into the edges of notebooks in class, the ones i wrote under my covers by the light of the moon. these words helped me become the person i am today. they belong to 5 year old me. 14 year old me. 19 year old me. now i am 25, a feat i owe to them for getting me through the roughest times in my life. there are many forms of love in this, some good, some bad, romantic, familial. there is hate disguised as love, love disguised as sadness, and love for oneself. this, i have found, is the most beautiful of all. and so, i will not erase them, and instead, attempt to embrace and love the me that i used to be. i want her words and emotions to be validated, and i am doing her a disservice if i do not. it is important to me to honor her before i do anything else. so here they are, and her and i will always be evergreen; not fully shedding our leaves until we acknowledge who we were, always belonging to each other somehow.

forever & always, keiran

a lament of love

barren land

in the dead of winter,
the cold and i long for you
with an ache i feel to the bone.

dans le mort
d'hiver
moi et le froid te
manques
avec une douleur je
ressens jusqu'à l'os.

scattered winds

it has been a year since i met you.
you came sweetly, carelessly.
you held a heart made of glass
and threw it to the wind,
thinking that if you just turned
around the shattered fragments
would not harm you.
doesn't it hurt? doesn't it cut deep
to know that you had something
real for once, and you broke it
in every way you possibly could?
the winds that brought you in
have carried my fragmented heart
to the ends of the earth,
and i will spend my days
searching endlessly
for the pieces of me
that i will never find.

songs of you

i awaken at the thought of you
i rise from my dreamland
at the sound of you calling
i would swim the oceans
for a lover who doesn't see me
sentiments spill out of lips
and cause trees to grow in your bones
to be Immortal!
to grasp onto the goddesses
and be carved into marble shrines
a name forgotten by lovers
and soon destined to haunt
the earth for eternity
remember me
i am here
i am Immortal to the page
can you hear me
i am here beside you
i am buried beside you

I AM CONSTANTLY BECOMING

everything except for you

i do not have you
your irresistible smile and emerald eyes
i do not have your hand in mine
or your arms holding me in the unbearable cold
i do not have your voice singing me
the sweetest love ballads in parking lots
or your lips kissing me goodnight
or early afternoon naps on silk bedding
i do not have any part of you
and somehow that feels like
i do not have anything
but i do have the sunshine
and ocean waves that fade into sunsets
i have autumn leaves and winter snows
peppermint tea and chilled cider
i have art and songs that aren't sung by you
i do not have you
but i have everything else
and that is more than enough

twisted shadows

you are picturesque in the garden we planted early spring. an assortment of things, all overgrown and wild. the tomato vines have almost taken over, but the smell is intoxicating so we don't mind it too much. you pluck a few and make your way over to the basil, it was always your favorite. i watch you breathe in deeply, trying to fill your lungs up with the earth. the sun shines down on you, but you seem to radiate just as much as she does, bringing life to this home. i like the way you look on me, how you reflect off of me. i seem better than i was before. before when there was no garden, no fresh basil or tomato for homemade pizza. before there was warmth, when the comfort came from the cold. before i felt the light, instead of only seeing it in my dreams. i am always scared of its return. it is always looming above me, around the corner. it's never there when i try to focus, but i know that it is. the darkness is always threatening to return. always threatening to fill up the spaces in between. as hard as i try, there will always be three of us in this bed. so, i watch you. and try hold on to it. try to memorize the edges like a photograph. a memory. when you leave it is all i will have. twisted around my bones like vines.

i have felt them - inspired by dickinson

i shall know peace
the sharp slant of a winter sunset
that spills through the trees
a wish on the first snowflake that lands on me
running until i can't catch my breath,
until i see the cliff side
and the tempestuous waves below
i shall find peace
through entangled limbs
of drooping apple trees
buried and dug up again out of frozen ground
a secret meeting among them in the orchard,
a secret that they'll keep
hushed whispers in the dead of night
a kiss in the darkness
i shall see peace
after the funeral of all the love we shared
before it was given to another
violets blooming when the last frost has gone
when there is midnight at noon
and i am blinded by its brilliance
when the moon returns to the night skies
i shall hear peace
a horse drawn carriage
that shimmers like the stars
i shall finally have a taste of peace,
when at last Death comes for me

fireworks

artists spin tales of gold and love
longing and loneliness
they paint pictures and build sculptures
all a dedication to the many faces of aphrodite
some write words to help ease their suffering
telling stories of heartbreak and misery
to remind the reader they are never alone
they'll tell a story of how i loved you
with everything i had in me
but it was a love that just couldn't be

a writer far greater than me
will make us immortal
and say how i did it to myself
how i always knew the ending
and still looked for the fireworks
i wonder what they'll know
we never spoke
about the mornings
i would wake up next to you
in the house by the lake
will they write about that?
about how i tried to change the ending?
how i clung to you like a child
holding desperately onto their favorite toy

i could've sworn i saw fireworks

the lovers

the dust settles on a love that once was ours. through golden peaks and violet heavens we loved with something not of this world and cried tears that flowered the gardens below. we built up cathedrals and castles and drank wine from frosted glasses. we soared through the skies on a dove's wings and watched ivy break through our marble dedications.

overgrown ruins replaced our utopia, a ghost replaced you. i ran through wilted gardens, looking for proof that we existed, but nothing grows here anymore except for thorns. lullabies turned into elegies, delicate skinned fruits rotted, and blue skies became grey. someone painted over our initials and even the ducks have found a new place to settle. we were here, i swear we were. weren't we just over there?

final apology

i have given you a million sorry's
a million apologies for something
i never asked for
you asked to kiss me
and i said yes
and i wish more than anything i hadn't
because i spent a year hating myself
for making you feel bad
because i couldn't give you what you wanted
i hated myself for your manipulations
how i tried so many times to leave
and it always ended with you crying
in my arms for hours
you'd tell me how you needed me
how i was the only one
then blamed me for not saying the same
i could never tell you i was in love
because i wasn't
how could i be in love with someone
who never really loved me
someone who tried to change me
who pushed my boundaries
until i no longer recognized myself
and didn't know what was best for me
until i had no choice but to stay
because i knew what would happen
every time i tried to leave
and choose myself

i was trying to be better
and i wished upon every star
it could be for you
but i always knew deep down
that i would never be better for you
because the person who i was meant to love
would not let me break myself
empty myself out
just to make room for them
i hate how i hated you at times
and still didn't have it in me to go
i hate how i still blame myself
like i led you on
even though you knew where i stood
like i broke you down
and paralyzed you
with manipulative tears
i'm sorry
for not having the strength to choose me
i'm sorry i blame myself
and i'm sorry i still blame you
i'm sorry that i lost myself
and let you break me
whether you meant to or not
i'm sorry that i still don't know
how to choose myself

stitched up carelessly

how could you not see the beauty in me
when i ripped myself open for you?
i pulled apart the fraying seams,
hoping you'd stitch them back up
carefully with your love and affection.
you asked to see me wholly,
to give every part of me
the love you thought i deserved.
what does it say about my goodness
that you touched me with poison
disguised as your love?

the valley

the evening was filled with empty wine bottles
and crumpled up parchment.
you picking the strings of your guitar,
singing me sweet songs.
there was a moment
in the darkness of the night,
in the dimly lit room,
where everything stood still.
you made your way to me,
every step enchanting,
captivating me in every movement you made.
here we made our dream world a reality,
a secret paradise for only us to know.
here, we fell in love.
we were heavenly,
and we hoped that the sun
would rebel the next morning
and decide to not show its face.
but it did, as it always does,
and we knew that with the rising
came the end of our story.

*i will never forget how you looked
in the morning sun, glowing and golden.
nothing has ever hurt so much.*

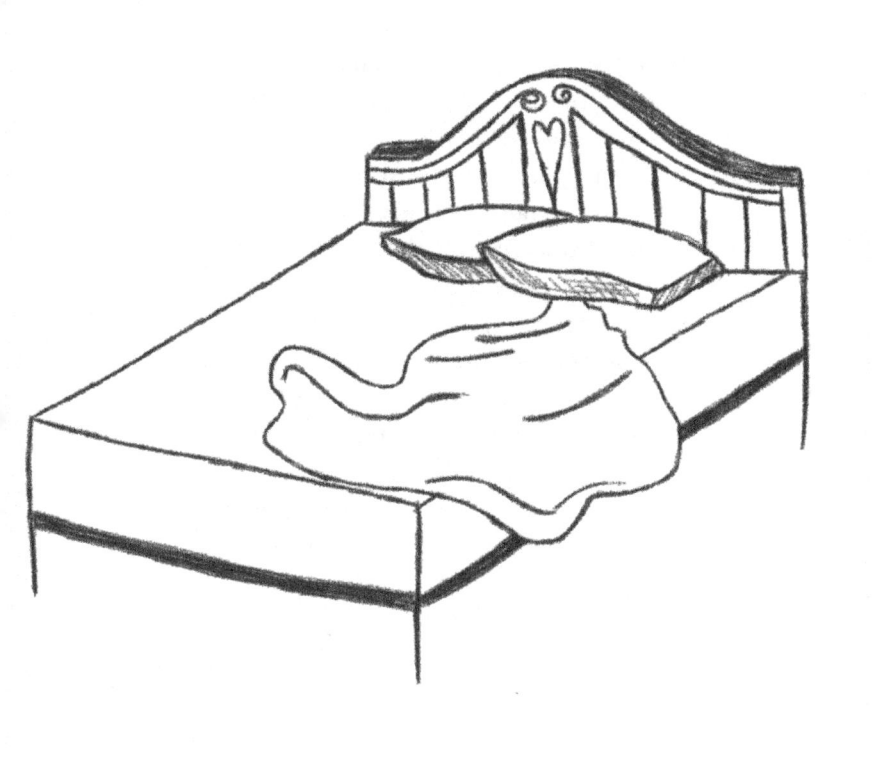

foreshadowing

i want to love you. when things get hard, i want to stay and not run. i want to kiss your fingertips and tell you that we will be okay because of the love we share. i want to build a home with you, to fill it up with warmth and love. i want to fall asleep in your arms and write you love letters to leave on the pillow the mornings you sleep in. if the desire i had for this life could conjure it into existence, it would already be ours. but it's not enough. it's never enough. i want you to know how hard it is for me to love and why i have always abandoned love so that when i ruin this, you will have known all along. perhaps it will not hurt as much this way, or at least i can tell myself that. if we give each other all of ourselves and then break, what will we have but fragments of a broken love that cut us too deeply? how do you recover from a lost love when you have given away all you are? i do not know how to love in a good way, and i am scared of hurting you before i learn.

revelation

i have found a revelation on your lips. i have never kissed someone like you. you have every intention of devouring me inside and out. to know and love every ounce of me without any conditions. you take my hands, never mind that they destroy all that they touch, and you try to create a holy place for us to belong to. liberate me from these man made chains, show me what it means to love in the holiest way possible. ignore the words written from those who wish to own the earth and heaven alike. the ones who would do anything in their power to have control do not possess this. they can not control this. try as hard as they might, they can not touch what was blessed by the gods. there is a revolution on your lips, a renaissance. there are poems and paintings and sculptures, orchestras and lyrics, stars and stories. but they can not touch us here.

herein lies our immortality: it lies in our love.

delusions

i hate how you called to me, beckoning me, like a siren. you didn't let me have a choice in my own life. you took away my free will. i am my parent's daughter through and through. i can hate you, but i can never leave. i can love you and wish that i had never met you. i used to wish that i could be good enough for you. i wished that i was not chaos contained and you were not in the line of fire. i wanted to be enough for you, for anyone. i wanted the love you had for me to make me want to stay. there is always a reason. i didn't listen to myself. i ignored when my gut told me to run. i inevitably hurt myself every time i ignore my feelings. this was not a great love. i was grieving a broken heart when i met you and you took advantage of me. i should've been stronger. you made me believe that i was the one hurting you, but didn't you see that i was dying inside every moment we were together? why couldn't you just let me go?

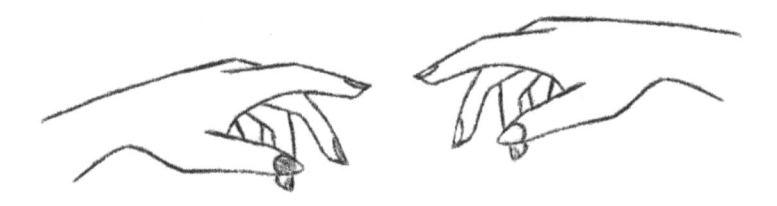

blue velvet

just a moment, i rest softly
a bed of moss and a blanket
of deep sapphire velvet
i breathe, too deep
the earth in my lungs
the stars in my belly
exhale, wooded smoke
crystals on my eyelids
just a moment, i rest softly
it begins here
the illusion of life
the dream of night
i rest softly
i rest softly
under her gaze
everything is okay
and so i sleep softly
for just a moment

love/paranoia

when you think of me
in the dark winter nights
undressed, music playing softly
in the candlelight
red wine lingering on my tongue
fingertips tracing constellations
do you feel the loneliness

picture me this way
in a never ending dream
sparking with embers
burning down everything
you think you know

illusory truth

i know that i never belonged to you, a bird far too carefree to ever bear chains, but the thoughts that keep me up in the night wonder if i was ever yours. burning questions that bleed onto the page, did you think you had me? counting up mistakes you thought i had made, a distraction from the faults that were your own. you needed space, you moved too quickly. i was water in your hands and did what i was told. you ran too far ahead and then jumped from the tracks, putting me in the lead. you pointed the blame, forgetting that i was still trying to find your place. i was never yours. i was never yours. god, how i wish i could've been. i think i was something to fill the spaces in the emptiness of your life. if i'm honest with myself, despite the back and forth and confessions of love, the signs were always there. i was never yours. i was never yours. god, how i wish i could've been.

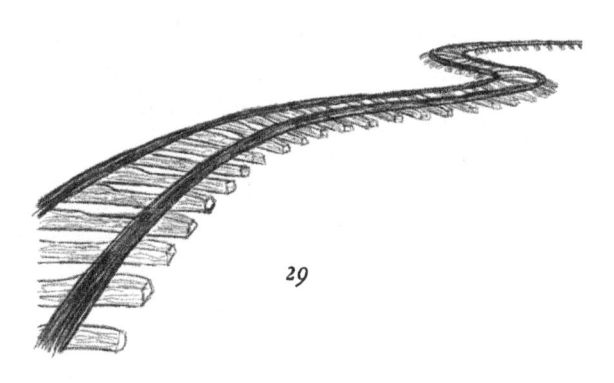

ghost

bound to me, tethered by that time and place. the ghost of you remains in my spine, hidden just out of reach. my unforgiving heart will be the death of me. my devotion to you, to what we could've been, the tie that binds. i twist and turn myself inside out, carving out the pieces of you, but your haunted graves still follow me wherever i go.

there has always been a darkness in me, and you clung to it like a moth to flame. you burned me, you burned us. you pulled poetry and prose from my withering body and used the pages to burn it all down.

i'm haunted. i'm haunted.

i wish you'd go, leave me to blow away the ashes on my own. eternal sunshine of the spotless mind my brain and put me on a train bound for nowhere, because anywhere is better than in your hands. i'd die just to be able to forget you. to forget how i opened up to you and allowed you to pour into me like the sunrise, like a waterfall. to forget the warmth on my face after the longest winter. to forget how we were like magic. a mirage. an illusion. a ghost.

liar, liar

white handprints on a black pullover
and honey hair tied back
clouds of flour in the air
thinly sliced apples
and cinnamon scented warmth
there's a piece of pastry dough
on the tip of your nose
but you don't mind
you are happy to just be here
doing something that feels cathartic
and also reminds you of home
you relive tales of your childhood
and i am happy just to be in your presence
you look at me with the most genuine smile
perhaps at the thought of a freshly baked pie
but maybe it is just meant for me
the smallest glimmer of hope
or maybe it's just my duplicitous nostalgia

i'll still have me

i watch the barren mountains turn to lush green velvet seemingly overnight, another summer that's beginning to pass me by without you. this summer feels different. it feels like it's carrying the weight of nostalgia in the form of my youth, absent is you and the weight of your calamity. i swim in rivers and sneak outside to watch the sunset, trying to capture the way the heat feels on my skin to save for the moments when i need it the most. the hard times that inevitably return.

somehow i will lose you, over and over again, but i will gain something far greater- me. i lost myself somewhere out there, leaving bits and pieces of my heart in the houses i lived in. so many bricks that belonged to so many buildings, not one of them a home. i looked for it for so long, every place that i've been, and i saw no signs of it. no hint of recognition, my soul could not feel the warmth of belonging.

i thought there was something wrong with me, that i could love someone so recklessly that i allowed them to fill me up, letting what fragments i had left of me drown. the thing about loving someone this way, so out of balance, is that you will be even emptier than you were to start with when they leave. i loved you. you left. paper thin, i blew away.
you walked away with all of you and what you thought were the best parts of me. but they were not. the best of me still belongs to me, and i will find it all on my own.

i thought i saw your face today

shortcut to the car / you dip down an alleyway / fingers red from frosted windows / turn the heat on / rest your eyes for a moment / autumn leaves / and warm air / fill the space between us / a train approaches / and you want to get on it / the car cuts off / and we race towards it / the train starts moving / you try to catch it / but you can't keep up / so you light a cigarette / i love you right now / and i'll never tell you this / 47 ways to guarantee love / though you loved me before / there was something about it / the guarantee / that scared you off / i'm running now / trying to catch up / i thought i saw your face / in one of the windows *i didn't love you, not really*

how many times must i write you out of me? how many half written poems and paintings will i start and never finish before i feel like you are finally out of me? ours was a story that should have never even begun. it does not matter how many times i rewrite our ending, it was never real. we were never real. a side reel shot of our kiss, removed from the final film, and i am left searching for you in every scene. half finished stories are your specialty, asking for clarification then getting lost in translation, i remember it all. you telling me you loved me, you saying that i felt too deeply for you. midnight Muse, but only when we argued; you wanted to believe that everything i wrote was about you. except, it wasn't. it never was. ours would've been a lovely book, the one i wanted to write. the one i tried to write. a fragment of reality- it was mostly a daydream of my desire for love. real love. but i didn't love you, not really.

i will learn to love my life

i fall in love every day, as many times as i breathe. i am reminded with each inhale what it is to feel my heart overflow with love. i am in love with the scent of warm cinnamon as the chilly october air rushes in through my window. lying on your bed wrapped up in blankets, no plans to do anything but embrace each others presence. the golden sunset dancing off of autumn leaves. a hazy pink winter sunrise when it's so cold i can see my breath. the smell of freshly unwrapped parchment and the first spill of ink on them. coffee shops filled with a beautiful assortment of strangers. twinkling lights visible from the street on a late december night. candle flickers casting shadows on the wall. the unknowing love of hundreds of people walking the downtown streets. libraries filled with thousands of stories, sheltered from the world outside. ballet slippers gliding across the stage. crackling records spinning and melding with the sound of a fireplace. a deep breath of icy air, cleansing me from the inside out. winter coats long discarded. footsteps in untouched blankets of snow. it is not the same love, but it is a love i need more than anything: the knowing of the world and how beautiful it is in the simple moments.

anatomy

*i feel like i need to cut open my chest
and use my own hands to rip it open
rummaging around,
searching for my heart
just to know
that it is beating*

*i need to feel my lungs
inflating,
breathing in
breathing out
to be certain*

that i am here.

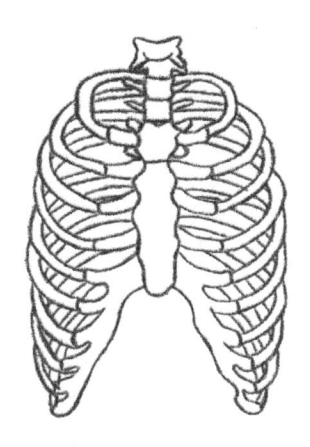

j.s.

*the last days of summer fade
into fall like the truest of romances
enveloping me in a gentle glow,
caressing me like new and familiar lovers
slowly settling on the breeze,
whispers of butterflies fluttering about
hues of autumn welcoming the warmth
into my body like i'd never before felt heat
the sun's rays beckoning her in all of her glory
sweet peaches linger on her fingertips
white wine dripping from her lips
like golden honey
drunk off of one sweet taste
brown eyes turning into golden flecks
of amber under the autumn sun
would have the richest man abandoning
his earthly possessions
glittering copper silk cascading down her back
mountains collapsing under her
if the earth shall fall
under her magical equinox touch,
then who am i to stand a chance?*

the sea

go left towards the sea, she said,
it matches my eyes.
she was right, i could see waves
crashing in them
and i was already drowning.
we walked down the rocky path
towards the shoreline,
and for a Midsummer night
it was cold, but that didn't stop you
from stripping down to your bare skin.
the silver moon made you shine
like you had been painted with diamonds.
i know the water was cold,
but you still pulled me in.
i don't know if it was the water
or your kiss that stopped my breathing,
but i could only stand there breathless,
unable to distinguish the icy blues and silvers
between your eyes, the moon, and the sea.
it was a painting i wish i could hang
behind my eyelids so i could see it in my dreams.

to be loved

i have cried into the midnight skies
more times than i can count.
begging the universe, pleading,
to give me the answers i seek.
what is the point in a taste of love
when it isn't real?
when the taste is so desirable
on my tongue, and bitter on theirs?
why give me a piece of what i yearn
for just to rip it away?
why must everything come at a price?
when i ask for love,
why can't i have it without any conditions?
i know everything happens for a reason,
but when i tell you my heart cannot
keep shattering, i mean it.
it cuts too deep and i fear i will bleed out
before i am whole again.
i know i must give myself the love i seek,
but why is it too much to ask
that someone else give it to me also?

in the most unlikely places

i didn't realize how much i had been holding inside, but it hit me this morning. my hands have been unable to write, the fear lingering in my fingertips. with you, the words flowed through them effortlessly, but you took it all. the magic, the love. you believed in me in a way that nobody ever had before. for better or worse, you were my Muse, the one who came to me every night in my mind, whispering poetry into my dreamscape. the good, the bad, the uncertainty- it was all there with you, and now it's gone. i know i must learn to stop pinning everything on one person. i know i must learn to let go and still keep the parts of me i thought only belonged to me when it was through the eyes of someone else. when i will finally be through reaching back into the past to find inspiration? when will i stop believing my words only possess magic when they're broken?

you always slip through my fingers

how could i ever have been able to grasp you,
even for a fleeting moment?
how could i have you again?
years and years later.
the sun is going down,
and the warm air holds a promise.
a promise of you.
of this moment.
we seem to be living in a photograph
and perhaps not actually here.
a hazy, grainy moment,
where everything stands still.
scared of taking a breath
and shattering the illusion.
how could i want you again
after all that we have been through?
did we go through it all
just to end up back in each other's arms?
you were a mirage, a memory, someone lost.
a blur, a hurricane, and the center
where everything was calm.
how could i have you again?
how could i take you back again?

and it feels like a stake through my heart

you told me that you'd never looked at a woman the way you looked at someone you met at the bar a few months ago. you said you'd never wanted so badly to take a woman home with you and make love to her in all the ways i wished you'd love me. i wanted you to want me the way you did her and sometimes, it felt like you did. but here it was, directly from you, spilling out of tirelessly truthful lips- you loved me but you didn't want me. i relive this again and again. you love me but you don't want me. confessing your love to me every moment you can, and i know now, finally, after all these years, that it doesn't matter. you can love me all you want, love me until the sun burns out, but you do not want me. what is the point in all of these confessions if you do not want me? what is the point in making me feel like there's a chance when you know there isn't? what does it bring you to make me think you are in love with me, even if you really are, when you will never want this? i am tired of telling myself the same painful truth over and over again. i am tired of you validating my instilled belief that i am not worthy of love. that love will always hurt me and i will never be good enough. i will always be desired, but i will never really be loved.

finding myself everywhere i go

i am searching for myself
i look for me in every passing face
every stranger on the street
has a part of me i'd like to be
i try to see bits and pieces
in cracks and crevices
i search the mountains
like they are my home
i look under every crashing wave
wondering if a part of me
the cold i feel constantly
is part of the february sea
i am searching for myself
and i found you
i did not find myself in you
but the you that you are
opened up a part of me
the one i saw momentarily
when i closed my eyes
but then you left me
and i thought i would drown
i thought i would never find myself again
i am still searching for myself
but no longer will i look in others
i will forever be a forager of myself
and i am learning that that is okay.

three years in may

delicate framed
and sweet clove on your mouth
you look at me
like you might devour me whole
you wrap your arm
around my waist so casually
like it was always meant to be
and kiss me softly

you kiss me more
you pull me in
you kiss me more
this is how you reignite
something that was once forgotten
you look at me like i am a painting
that's just waiting to be made
you inhale deeply
sweet smoke disappears
you pull me in
and make magic
from what lingers
in the air

mind over *matter*

ivy broke into my rib cage
and grew around my bones,
squeezing my heart
until every sadness poured out.
it dripped down my fingers,
and onto the page,
because finally, my mind had no say.

release them. release them.

"feel the weight lift off of your shoulders
as you unburden yourself of the things
long buried. you have always been the key.
a garden grows inside of you."

re: my current feelings

i don't want to do this with you again, this cycle we keep finding ourselves in. you love me or you don't, you love me but you never did, you love me and you always have. the agonizing pain i feel every time you go away, the tearing of our strings tied around my spine. my unforgiving heart and precarious mind, i have yet to tell you to leave and actually mean it. i have yet to tell you that i have missed you and not fear it scaring you off.

you love me, you don't. maybe you will, maybe you won't. i am unafraid of most things, but i am scared of losing you. the only weakness i have ever felt is spilling my heart out to you on the page, pinning all of my hopes to your hands and praying i don't slip through your fingers, daring to dream about a future we could have if you wanted. but i don't believe in "if they wanted to, they would" because sometimes they can't. you love me, but you can't. the truth is this- i want to feel. you bring forth the poetry in my body and i write until my hands bleed, but the pain of losing you and loving you over and over again, in my words, in my arms, is too much. i miss you but i won't, i love you but i can't.

will i ever leave this dead end town / journal entry

i feel it again. the overwhelming desire to run. to get as far away as i possibly can. why is it that i do not feel as if i can stay in one place for long? for someone who is scared of change, i crave the difference of another place. my bones long for far away mountains and oceans, the familiarity of cities i don't know. they call to me, and i wonder what is holding me back. i will blame my lack of money, which is not entirely wrong, my job, my obligations, but the truth is that it is my fear holding me back. the unknown. all of the things that could go wrong. all of the things that could go right. i desire more. i need more. i do not have the luxury to seek more. i feel it constantly like a hunger. i do not think it will let me rest until i have a taste. i am scared of dying here, of having never done the things i wanted to.

dawn

i find no beauty in mankind,
none that i shall love
in the depths of my soul.
what could there be within them
more beautiful than poetry or mountains?
oceans and autumns?
the first snow in winter or sunsets and sunrises?
i have never been able to name such a thing.
my eyes have never seen it.

nature's diary

i drown in the ocean and then hang myself upside down from the crescent moon. sea foam turns into clouds and the sky becomes an ocean. stars become their own reflections on waves and all of the things that have ever existed, simultaneously never have. i dream at night about a life i never had and think it into existence in a parallel reality. i sing myself to sleep with a song from a 3000 year old tree. i used to think the earth was here because of me, that without my eyes it wouldn't be here. but the beauty of nature is that it exists whether or not i do. it is here for me when i need it, like a mother comforting a child, but it is not here *because* i need it. it holds all of the truths that have ever happened and everything that will ever come to pass. the earth sings ancient songs that my ears simply cannot hear because they are not meant for me. i cannot conduct an orchestra and not know what is playing. i am an observer. i'm here to get lost in it, to disappear and come out better than i was before, to see my life more clearly. i am here to exist in alignment with nature and nothing more.

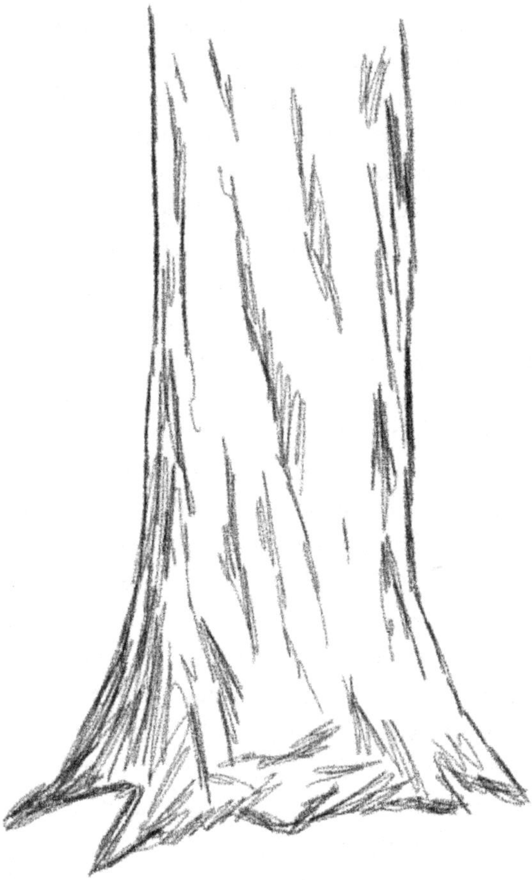

an ode to autumn and home

i miss the feeling of parchment under my fingertips. the way my pen glides across the page with the ease of a ballet rehearsed day in and day out. i miss the creaking floor at 6 am, the sound and smell of coffee brewing while the cool october air rushes in through an open window. i can still see the sun rising over the top of the mountain while i sit there in the earth's silence, more at peace than i've ever been. this is a feeling of belonging, it's the home for which i long. my favorite autumn reminiscent tunes play softly in the background. i miss the feeling in my chest as i run along the road hidden by trees, how nature seemed to be waiting for me. i miss waking up before the sun and walking the trail beside my house, long before the rest of the world would wake. i miss how it felt to be my own person, to finally have a taste of who i am and who i would become. i miss the freedom. i miss the crackling fire of a burning candle, piano songs filling my ears, the wind rustling the papers i had long forgotten. when i think of old homes and candlelit rooms, i am nostalgic for a feeling. the record player stops spinning, and for a moment, just one single moment, i am home.

this is an ode to autumn and home. the only time i've ever felt at home in the places i've lived is when the leaves began to change. i deeply long for the home in which i no longer live, a place i'd give anything for. to whomever occupies my space, i hope you appreciate it as much as i did. i hope that when the cold weather sets in and you sit out on that creaky front porch, tea and book in hand, that you feel all the love and happiness i ever felt, and may it bring you a sense of belonging and serenity.

view from apartment 10

THERE GREW AROUND ME / A LABYRINTH OF ROSES / WANTING TO CARRY ME AWAY / THEY FELT WITHIN ME MY DESIRE / TO DISCOVER ALL THAT THERE WAS IN THIS UNIVERSE / AND THE NEXT / TO SEE WHAT HAD NEVER BEEN SEEN / TO HEAR SYMPHONIES / LOST AT THE HANDS OF TIME / TO TASTE THE DANGEROUS / FORBIDDEN FRUIT / THEY NEEDED TO SHOW ME / THAT I WOULD NOT BREAK / TO TEACH ME TO ROOT MYSELF / WHERE I STOOD / TO GO WHERE I WANTED / TO GO / THERE GREW WITHIN ME / A LABYRINTH OF ROSES / AND I HAPPILY LOST MYSELF IN THERE / IN ORDER TO FIND MY TRUTH

sometimes a mountain is just a mountain

and it always seems daunting at first
you know you have to climb it
but it's hard
so you camp out at the bottom
hoping that if you wait long enough
the earth will have moved it for you
or maybe it'll get worn down
by all the others who must cross
so you sit
and you wait
and you watch everyone else pass you by
sometimes they stop for a bit
weary from the journey thus far
but one day they'll pack their bags
and you'll watch them grow smaller
in the distance
as you remain in the same spot
you were in years ago
and maybe it isn't fair
a tale as old as time
the universe will listen to you
and comfort you
and guide you
but nobody can move the mountain for you

one day you'll start
and it will feel like
you're not making any progress
each mountain the same as the last
slowly but surely
you'll see a glimmer of hope
you'll see that the place you used to belong to
seems a bit further away than it had yesterday
so you climb and you climb
and you'll climb it once more
then it will seem like you're back
where you began but somewhere
you find the strength to try again
and somehow the mountain seems less scary
and again and again and again
every time you climb the mountain
it gets smaller until one day it's just a hill
and you'll look back and see
hundreds of identical mountains,
each less daunting than the last,
and you'll know that you did it
nobody moved the mountain for you

new year's resolutions

i wish to gain a new perspective, to see the world through the eyes of a creature less severe than me. i wish to belong to the rivers and the trees, to float upon the wind like a feather. to be so gentle and still be able to take on the world. when you think of me, where else could i be but on the mountainside? dangling from a branch like i used to do in the days of my youth. i want to look at the world and hear the way the earth speaks, for she is always giving us her wisdom. i'd like to sing songs and stop when the bluebirds begin, always learning something new. i think that a bed of moss would be perfectly lovely right now, covered up with a blanket of night, and creating new constellations in the stars with my fingertips. i long to see the cities and lights fall away out of my vision to make room for thousand year old woods and rocky cliff sides. i wish to walk amongst the violets until the end of the road, and when i get there, find a new place to roam.

a requiem of remembrance

i never lost it

when i was a child, i used to spend all of my days outside. as i grew older, day by day, my childhood slipped away from me. there's the inevitable nature of simply growing older, no one can escape the tolls of time, but also having to be so mature at such a young age. i lost my inner child, and i lost my connection with nature. i have spent these last few months trying to work on myself and heal my younger self. my desire is to get back a piece of my innocence that was lost, to find my purpose through healing myself and rediscover nature. i can't change the past, but it's never too late to be a kid again, to love blindly and fully, and find the magic that i used to have.

the weight of the unknown

i fear i know nothing, and how can i? to live in fear with a heart that thrives in solitude? what can i know? this earth is vast and i do not know her. i have grown and not placed roots for the knowledge that was passed down to me. and so, have i truly not grown? the burden that is not mine to bear is a simple one. the burden is this- you are only going to know these valleys and hills. it is the burden of not knowing if you will ever know or do all that you are supposed to.

be of good heart

i never learned how to trust the thing that was beating inside of my own chest.

abandoned houses

this place hasn't felt like home for a while,
not like it did in the beginning.
in the beginning, there was sunshine
and smiles and hope.
now this place surrounds me like a tomb,
holding me in with no way out.
the floors creak and moan,
i can hear the wind whistling
through my cracked bedroom window,
beckoning me into the night.
i no longer feel like i can breathe while i am here.
you left so long ago,
but remnants of you still remain
in the cracks and crevices in the walls.
as i am packing my belongings
i will plant seeds in them
so the next people who live where your ghost
remains won't see anything but a beautiful garden.
they will water them and flourish,
and i will have moved my garden to a new
location, one that only exists in my dreams.
i will make it into a beautiful place, with walls so
high that you could never find a way in,
and so that my flowers never find their way out.

i am my own worst enemy

perhaps it is true that my words
may sometimes hurt others
but more often than not,
it is my own pen turned dagger
that i have found in my chest.

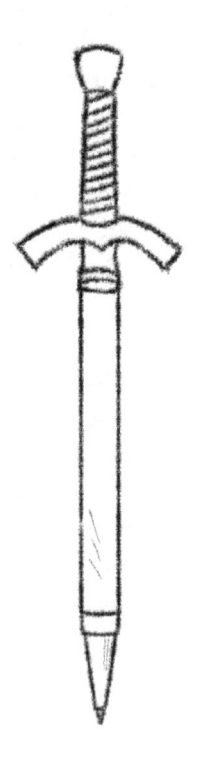

paralyzed

we had all of these plans for our life together.
now everything has changed
and i'd give anything to redo the past year.
nothing is the same, we are not the same.
how would you react if i called you
and told you everything i was feeling?
    i miss you
    i want you back in my life
    can we pick up where we left off?
    can we drop everything
    and move across the country?
we could do anything as long as it was us.
but there is no us
and i feel as though i can't do anything.

never be the same

and there we were, as if we had never been, as if we'd always had. a familiar stranger before my eyes, one with shorter hair but the same sense of humor and dark brown eyes. your eyes flickering back and forth, desperate to avoid mine from across the booth. the waitress allowed a momentary escape from the prison we had built at this table, and the walls were back up as soon as she had left. there was so much to say, but quite possibly no way to say it. a longing to rekindle, but no person willing to be the first to break. and who should have to? which one says i'm sorry? how do i forgive you when there were so many unforgivable things? things that you ignore into nothingness? should i say i'm sorry for being hurt? do you say i'm sorry when we both know you've never meant it?

"more coffee?"

"just the check, please."

3:42 am

there's still a bit of time before i'm supposed to be up, but i haven't slept a full night in ages. i cling desperately to sleep, hoping to slip back into a world that is not my own, whether i remember it or not. last night i dreamt there were rattlesnakes in my house and i worry what that means for my sister. i looked up the significance of them and from what i gather, it means a toxic situation within your own home. i watch as she loses pieces of herself in the worst kind of person, knowing there's nothing i can do to stop her. i sometimes feel as though i am slipping away too, teetering constantly on the edge of safety and going insane, and risk and insanity. these sound the same, but going insane means being stuck in cycle i've been in for years, and insanity means going after what i truly want, and that thought is terrifying. i know she feels it too, the yearning, the itch. maybe this is enough to make me take the risk. the knowing that if i jump, she will too. once she sees what is possible, she will know that she can do anything. we have always had a hard time in believing something we haven't yet seen.

like my mother

maybe i am not capable of sitting still
because my mother is not. she too is always
running towards the next thing, or away from
something, someone. i look at love like it is
something to be feared, like it will destroy me.
so i run, just as my mother always has. i run back
into the arms of ones who would never love me,
who will always give me less than i deserve.
sometimes i think the only difference between my
mother and i is that my desire to run towards
happiness and hopes and dreams is stronger than
hers. but i sit here, writing words that will never
see the light of day, and i wonder if this is even
true. a dream is just that, it isn't real. i am sure my
mother has many dreams that i don't know about,
but sometimes life gets in the way. i wish that i
could teach us both that it's okay to be selfish
sometimes and it's okay to take chances on real
happiness, that it's okay to be afraid.

the hum

sometimes i think that one day i'll shatter too hard and i'll no longer exist. that there is a hum the whole world can hear except for me and i'll spend my entire life trying to listen, pressing my ear against a brick wall, only to discover that it was my own thoughts preventing it from flooding inside of me. sometimes i think the sky must be a different color, but nobody wants to be the one to tell me that things are not as i think they are, and sometimes that's okay. sometimes the ocean gets too heavy and falls from the sky, it cracks and shatters just like i do and it ceases to exist. then out of nowhere i awaken and find myself floating along, unsure of how i got there to begin with. the only home i've ever known exists in my mind, and she is a frightening thing to behold. i would not wish this upon anyone, the inability to hear the hum, the inability to change what's around you.

i want to be a feeling

i want to be warmth. i want to be freshly brewed tea on a rainy afternoon or hot cocoa by the fire place. i want to be a dark and rainy forest in the middle of nowhere, untouched by the hands of time. i want to exist in the first glance of new lovers, in the breath before a first kiss. the spark of a match, just before the fire begins. the change in the weather just before the clouds begin to form. i want to be the simple moments that make up a beautiful life. i want my days to be filled with it. the longing. the love. the anger. the fire. the passion. the desire. the hope. the tears. the misery. i want it all. i want to be it all.

about the letter you found that i wrote

do you know what you're teaching us as we watch you bend over backwards for a man who can't be bothered to lift a finger to help you? a man who tears you down with every chance he gets? what are we supposed to know about love when you loved a man who destroyed your soul for 12 years? a man who hurt you, time after time, who was then succeeded by a man who continued that sacred tradition of seeing just how far you'd bend before breaking. aren't we supposed to learn from your mistakes? aren't you? how am i supposed to love someone and let them love me when the only love i've ever seen was disguised as poison? don't you know that she will watch you, not even a teenager, fight to occupy a space you don't even want? what does this teach my brother about how to love a woman? that it's okay to abuse them, because she will always take it and she will always stay? what does this teach my sister? don't you know she will follow in your footsteps? she will love someone who shows their love through anger and fists and you will be sure to mention that it is not your fault. all i have learned is that perhaps it's better to not love at all. but you will always tell me it isn't your fault, as if somehow at 14 i could know that what i see in my life is not how it should be. that it will not always be like this.

a light to cut through the darkness?

the weight is enough to crush you. the loneliness could kill you. the silence that you retreat into to feel whole again is the same silence that is too loud, too dark to let the flowers inside. they try to make their way in every now and then, but these walls are too strong.

the urge to cut everything off, the sights, the sounds, the people, is persistent, knocking on your door all throughout the day. you may have been able to avoid it today, but you know that soon enough it will be back, as eager to guide you into darkness as it ever was.

i believe that i could be a garden, roses climbing up and down the walls, their flesh fragrant and intoxicating in the lilac evening. ivy twisting and turning over marble fountains, waters the color of sapphires running through the land. there could be a willow tree dancing in the wind like it was performing a ballet. the wooden swing sways softly, inviting.

a secret place where i could be happy, i could be home. i ache for a place like this. i will scream it into the black midnight sky, crying until i fear i will never cry again.

but darkness is a powerful thing. nothing to be seen or heard for miles. it's impossible to know which way is up or down, or if i'll ever make it out of this place.

forcing yourself into the light will do more harm than good as it wears you down, little by little. pretending like nothing is wrong is a nice temporary bandaid until the late night crying weakens the bind.

what is there to do? how do you find your way out of the maze with nothing to guide you? how do you make yourself heard when you lost your voice years ago? how do you turn on the light?

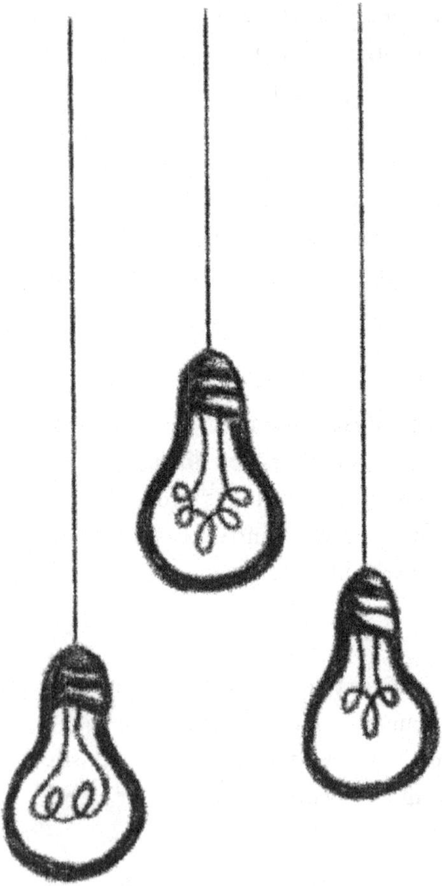

family values

do not preach family values to me
when you are slowly killing yourself,
ruining any chance at a family we could be.

holiday hell part I

i pull into the deserted gas station and get out of the car. the wind blows sharply and it makes me wrap my coat a bit tighter around my body. though it has gotten chillier throughout the day, i can't help but note that it isn't as cold as it usually is. i am standing there, trying not to cry, and i know from inside the car, she is doing the same thing. we are tired, and we are angry. and you, you are the same as you always are- drunk.

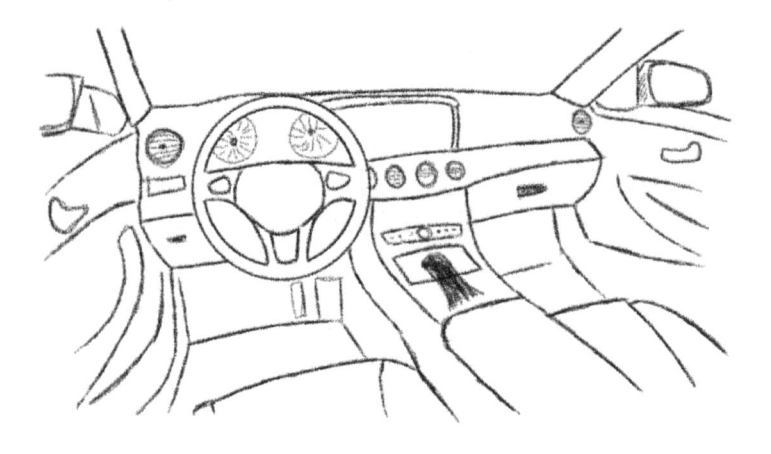

holiday hell part II

she hangs up the phone and i can tell she is frustrated and i don't know why. i assume it has something to do with the person on the other end of the line, but it doesn't. she finally peeks open, bitter words that are sharp on her tongue and the tears come with them. everything that i had been trying to hold back came out too and we cried together in silence. we cried like we had just left the funeral of someone we loved. with as much as he drank today, and every other day, we knew that the funeral would come sooner than later. we knew that there could never be enough time to love those around you, that it would never be too much to try and repair those relationships. all he was doing was ticking off days faster and faster, pretending like nothing was wrong.

i know nothing about you

i want to get to know you.
i want to know about your childhood.
what did you enjoy doing?
who was your best friend?
did you fight with your siblings,
the way i do with mine?
did you ever strive for your father's attention,
needing his approval like the air in your lungs?
like i do with you?
who was your first love?
when you met the woman you would marry, why?
why was she different than the first two?
why did you love my mother?
what are the moments in your life that you'll
remember the day you die?
what are your dreams?
your aspirations?
you are still so young,
but i can't get to know you
because i'm scared.
what is the point in getting to know you
when someday soon you will die,
and it will have been your own fault?
how do i find it in me to think
that it's okay for you to do?
how do i find it in me to love you?

catharsis

you are the one subject i've always found it difficult to write about. i have momentary lapses, ones where i let my emotions show. that is where my writing lives, in the cracks i've let show. for just a brief moment. but you, you are something i never let slip. you see, writing is cathartic, but writing something down, something you've been hiding, makes it more real. you have to accept the things you buried deep inside of you and tried so desperately to make into nothing. it is what you have done, it is what you have taught me, and it is what i have done with every emotion i've ever felt.

please find your way back

i am so angry at you.
this is the very first emotion
that comes to mind
when i think of you.
how could you do this to me?
to us?
and then, i am sad
because i don't want to
ever picture my life without you,
and it's all i seem to be doing lately.
i want to help you,
but you have given up on yourself.

monsters under my bed

the way that you treat us when you are drunk is abuse. the slurring cuss words, the easily taunted anger. the monsters that used to haunt my dreams as a child bore your face. red and angry, alcohol pouring from your body as if it had replaced the water in you. do you not recall the days of your childhood, your father indifferent to his children? instead, finding all he needed at the bottom of a bottle. you are supposed to be different. i know you loved him, but you are not supposed to mimic him. you are supposed to be better. you are not supposed to hit your wife, or your children until they think that this is all there will ever be in life. until all they feel for you is fear. you are not supposed to find peace, especially if that solace was found in the arms of another woman, while your wife was at home taking care of the kids. the ones that you have always been indifferent to. you are not supposed to treat your kids like a bill that you reluctantly pay, like you didn't know what you were signing up for. you are not supposed to be mad when they don't want to come over because when they do, all you do is try and make them feel guilty and drink yourself to death.

the summer he left

i miss the sticky sweet of his absence
the suffocating august air was hot
but i don't remember it
being something i found unpleasant
that whole time feels like going outside
and feeling the sunlight against your skin
after lying in the winter snow
warm and inviting with its touch

"come here and i will love you always, i will never burn you with my touch"

the fall he returned

and then he was back
and the sun beating down
against my face felt like betrayal
you felt like one
everything you did and said felt like betrayal
still, i couldn't find it in me
to blame you
so i blamed the sun
she, in all her bright,
beautiful glory burned me
like she was chained to your deception
the flames took the air from my lungs
and you were left standing
in a pile of ashes alone

"if you don't learn from your mistakes, you'll end up like icarus- nothing"

love is always pain

she was just a kid, ignorant to the shadow hiding behind the door; the one who tells her she will do whatever she has to do just to feel something. now to be 18, she doesn't know when to put up a fight. you didn't tell her how it would feel, so the way that he grabs her wrists, it feels like home somehow. the way he won't let go feels like the love she knew in her youth. two decades worth of blurring the lines and she can't tell when something is wrong. she can't tell if love is supposed to leave bruises the way it does or if love means doing the things that she doesn't want to do. you made her too old in her youth, you made her bite her tongue when she needed to scream out. you made her believe that no was not something she could ever say. you made her believe that love isn't a love unless it causes pain.

january 2018

even far beyond the confines of the state in which you were held- nothing had changed. you were still the same person you had always been. separation of man and a new location won't fix something that was broken way before those things made me objective. i foolishly thought things would change. that you would suddenly be better and this brokenness we all feel would glue itself back together.

i was wrong.

peace in solitude

we have a lot in common
we could talk from dusk until dawn
but when the sun rises
and no longer am i surprised
it is gone
something has gone wrong
it is me, not you, i promise
nothing to make a compromise
i'd just rather watch the sunrise
alone

endless waiting

i am doomed to a life of waiting.
for the perfect moment,
opportunity,
person.
i am waiting for the perfect sunset,
or the weather to turn cold.
the first snow.
the first bloom.
i am always waiting.
for life to give me lemonade
instead of lemons.
for love to find me.
for my dreams
to become reality.
but what do i do
while i wait?
i spend my days
counting the minutes
while wasting them away.
then hating that i wasted them.
so again i count up to the days
when i no longer have to wait
and it is a very cruel cycle
that i have put myself in.

i want love, not apologies

i have seen my mother suffocate in the hands of men under the guise of love. i have seen her soul wear thin and bend backwards until it snapped and it shattered. i have seen her shoved backwards until she fell to the ground. i have heard her scream and cry until all of the breath in her lungs was filled to the brim with fear and loathing. and maybe she didn't mean to but it had to come out some way so she breathed it over us and we learned to have fear and loathing. sometimes she loved us so much that she showed it in the way he did. i know she never meant it, but now when someone shows me love i feel like i can't breathe because i want my lungs to be filled with rose buds and rivers, not poison spilling from them to me. i want someone's hand in mine, not around my throat. i want love, not apologies.

it's taken me a long time to realize that love and fear do not belong in the same hands and love should pour from them to you and just because they love you does not mean they're allowed to hurt you.

the days of our youth

the days of our youth have come and gone
summer days spent foraging for wild blackberries
staining our mouths and fingertips a bright violet
laughing uncontrollably and chasing each other
until we came tumbling down to the ground
out of breath and free
collecting rocks and leaves
trying to mimic the songs of birds
we haven't been close since those days
but i miss who we used to be
sisters and friends
the briefest of years when you were my protector
the one who would always watch out for me
the one who was always there for me
when our mom and dad couldn't be
i used to blame you for leaving
for finding your way out and taking it
without a glance back at me
it felt like you had abandoned me
but now i understand that you didn't
you just did what you had to do for you
and i know that you'd do it over again
just as i know that i would make the same choice
i would do anything to feel as free as we used to

mirror image

i wish i could love you, or i wish i didn't care. this in between will be the death of me. torn between not wanting to get too close and knowing that i would cross oceans to help you heal. it's hard to hate you. you only turned out this way because of your own parents and it's so hard to know what to do when you're the one holding your family together. trust me, i know. but you know things are broken. it's okay to hate your mom and dad for they did. it's okay to grieve someone who wasn't there. can you not see the symmetrical reflection of your relationship with them and the one you have with us? it's a mirror dream. your dad on one side and you on the other, mimicking his moves.

through the seasons

you seemed to grow as effortless as the seasons
you began so small and so quickly you grew
the rain washed away your insecurities
and the sun brought a new you
but so fast you seemed to weaken
with autumn's chill
and by winter i didn't recognize you
they filled your head with thoughts so cold
and dangerous
you seemed almost willing to believe them
and your light began to fade

stop letting the opinions of others
change how you view yourself
you will make it out of the cold
and you will feel the sunshine once again

a book of you

if i'd let myself, i could write a book of you
fill the pages with things you used to do
i could write you into verses
etch you into parchment
use your spine to create the backbone of the book
your raven colored hair as ink,
your skin like the pages it holds
i could fill it with your history, our history,
with the way you've grown into the person you are
i know if your mom could ever get over herself
she would be so proud
i'd dedicate it to 13 year old you
who used to clean up after her mom,
the girl who had the best parts of her picked out
like weeds from a garden
that girl was so hopeless
she is the one you need to make proud
the you who grew up too soon
the you who tried her very best
despite her world telling her that she couldn't
i hope it would be a book that she would see
sitting upon a dusty shelf
and read when the nights seem to never end

exhaustion

i am tired. not the kind of tired you feel when you are in the car for too long or how your eyes are drowsy from reading novels. my body is weighed down with exhaustion, my bones are laced with an uncertain deprivation. the kind of tired you feel when the weight of emotions becomes too much to bear. when your mind is a constant string of thoughts that have no true meaning and your heart is full of sadness and anxiety, but your fingers can not seem to rest because if they stop then you will have to step back and take a look at the world around you. if you do that then you will feel alive, and if you feel alive, truly alive, then you wonder why you can not feel the things you are meant to be feeling. when my mind is quiet i am anxious and i am doubtful. when my mind is too quiet i tend to create distance because i can not feel the presence of others. i feel small and i feel how it is to not belong to anyone or anything or anywhere flow through me. it is not a river of naivety that i had hoped for, it is an ocean of bad emotions and all it does is rock me back and forth until i am fast asleep.

all the times you prayed

i pull the photo album from the white bookshelf, its leather binding dusty and worn from decades of use. it has been a long time since the original photos were in there. what was once kept inside has found its way out, secret memories forgotten, replaced now with what pictures i could find of me as a child and it almost fills it entirely. tucked away in the back are memories of old friends, photo booth clips and touristy attractions. i flip through the pages and see me at 3 years old, happy and unassuming. i see a little girl who was timid and camera shy, she had already been through things she shouldn't have had to. i see me at 5 years old, still clinging to the same sad smile i'd carry into my teenage years. the photographs are tainted now. the happy memories, the smiling pictures of my parents are replaced with ghost stories. i know the moments not captured were ones of bad dreams. i try to look at them and remember late night ice cream and 90's sitcoms, but it's muddled with late night fighting and lying in bed, wishing, praying for once i could just sleep through it. maybe that's why i have such a hard time sleeping now. maybe one day i will be able to look at the pictures and not be reminded of the poison spilling out behind the lens.

the ocean has always accepted my sadness

i'm reminded of that day
by the sand stuck in the lines of my shoes
each grain a reminder
of the icy waves crashing into the shore
i can almost feel the late afternoon sun
warm against my cheeks,
battling against the january wind
i watch the people come and go,
the seagulls desperately trying to escape the cold
but i am just fine in my solitude,
welcoming the freezing ocean
in all of its magnificence
nothing has ever felt more like home.

brick & mortar

how many times must i tear myself down to help build you back up? you destroy yourself in the hands of unholy men in a futile attempt to make up for the lack of affection from your father. he spent his days destroying you, teaching you to be mortar, holding together a broken home. this is what you have taught me as well. that it does not matter what harm is done to me, i will hold my head up high and do what i must to bring back the peace. you taught me to be the caretaker of the house. to raise your children as my own. to do the best i can. to comfort my parents when they feel guilty for the pain they caused me because they didn't mean it. they love me, of course they didn't mean it. i know you never meant it.

i exist too much

sometimes, i exist too much.
and other times i am an empty house,
full of ghosts and memories
that i don't even remember.
i exist within my space
and in the place of others,
but i am nowhere in between.
nowhere to be found.
i am the weight of calamity,
and i am a sink overflowing.
i am too much sometimes.
but sometimes not enough.
never in between.
i am loved,
but not wanted.
i am wanted,
but not needed.
i am too much.
i will bottle it up.
i will disappear.
i am a ghost.
i exist too much.
i will cease to exist at all.

i am

you can find me where the ocean meets the sky
the line where the earth stops
i am the place where the sun drowns itself
where the moon comes up for air
i am the ferocious winter winds
icy as the unrestrained waters it kisses

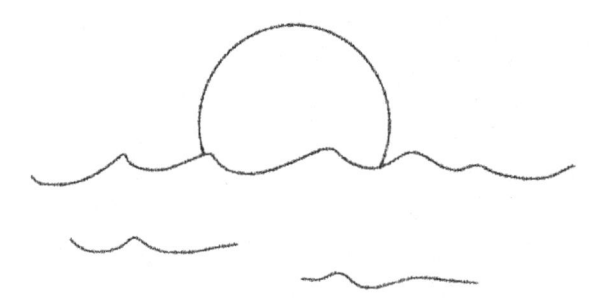

i hate this part of texas / the tavern

there's a restaurant i pass when i go driving late at night that's been open since 1930. i used to go all the time when i was a kid. my grandfather would take me with him to run errands and we would go every time. i'd sit proudly atop a bar stool much too high for my 5 year old legs, and feel a sense of accomplishment that i could even reach the countertops. such a simple time. happily sitting there amongst the regulars, pretending like i belonged with this crowd. they would always cheer me on, no matter what i did or said. i was happy. i like to think that on his good days, my grandfather used to take my mother here too and she would sit there in the same way, in the same seat, boastful and content. feeling grown up and wishing she would always feel this way- on top of the world and loved. i hope she still feels that way.

persephone

perhaps she is the spring blowing in,
bringing life in her wake
she causes the flowers to rise
out of even the most dark and scary places
she dances in the april showers
as if it was some innate thing inside her
something she could never tire of
perhaps she is the summer
blistering heat, sparking fire
if you dare get too close
maybe her eyes spark like fire
she is the reason that the lands will flourish
when the leaves begin to change,
the fire in her eyes may die,
the flowers may begin to wilt
with saturated lips and red stained skin,
she retreats to the home she's always known
only she knows if she finds joy
after all, if anyone could find
the light it would be her
adorned in the darkest of colors
a forbidden fruit crushed
between her delicate hands
she will repeat this dance
for evermore until the end of eternity
she is made of darkness,
but she is also made of light

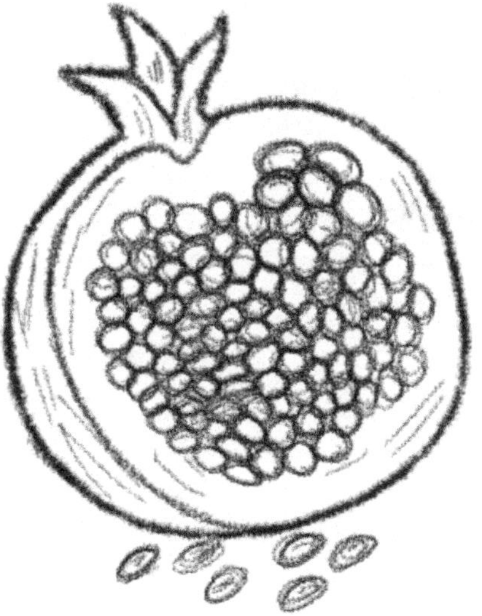

summer

i loved you
in the warmth of summer
you kissed me three times
and promised a love
to write poems about
confessions of heart
and glittering fields
blackberry wine
and hope dangling cliffside
drowning in the river below
you loved me
i swear you did
you kissed me
i swear i can feel it
even now
here in the cold

fall

i loved you
in the deep saturation of fall
friends to lovers
two times over
reeling from heartbreak
a mindless distraction
i loved you
and i loved you
until i didn't
or i never did
three years of talking about it
and it never came to pass
until a night in october
but i was thinking of someone else
i swear she was there

winter

you loved me
in the bitter winter
and made me believe
that i was meant to love you too
i searched for forgiveness in the stars
for the pain i caused you
when i tried to leave
i searched for recompense
for the sins i made against my body
my empathy will be the death of me
or is it the result of my childhood
to break down every action
until i am frozen with fear
scared to upset you in the slightest
i hated me
i wished that i didn't exist
i wished that i could turn the hands of time
to go back to the first time
and never notice you at all

spring

it was in the solemn spring
that i discovered the love i had
for me and all that i was
i set out to discover
everything that i could become
to find the life that i wanted
to do things that brought me joy
joy that i had not felt since my youth
i forgave myself for letting go
of all the emotional weight
that was not mine to carry
i began the fool's journey
into the forest
of my soul
to heal from the inside out
i let go of everything
that i was not supposed to be
and let nature take over

a thank you & dedication

thank you for reading my words. thank you for giving me the space to release the words i have been carrying for so long. it has always been my dream to do this, and now i have. twice.

thank you so much to ann-sofie vejs for the most beautiful, magical, breathtaking cover a person could ever dream of having. IG: @annsofievejs.illustration

thank you to salem paige for doing my french translation (so if it's wrong it's their fault <3). IG: @corpseofapoet

this book is dedicated to me, in every year of my life, but also to my sister. we have not had the easiest time and we certainly were not close for most of our lives. in the recent years, we managed to find an actual sisterhood, one that i always dreamed we could have. i'm sorry that it took us so long, but i am here for you. always. most of these words were written when i was your age, and i hope that this helps you find a way to release all of your own words one day, and i'll be there every step of the way to help however i can.

a lament of love index

an ode to autumn and home - 54
anatomy - 37
and it feels like a... - 45
barren land - 10
blue velvet - 27
dawn - 51
delusions - 26
everything except for you - 14
final apology - 19
finding myself everywhere i go - 46
fireworks - 17
foreshadowing - 24
ghost - 30
i didn't love you, not really - 35
i have felt them - 16
i thought i saw your face today - 34
i will learn to love my life - 36
i'll still have me - 32
illusory truth - 29
in the most unlikely places - 43
j.s. - 39

liar, liar - 31
love/paranoia - 28
mind over matter - 48
nature's diary - 52
new year's resolutions - 60
re: my current feelings - 49
revelation - 25
scattered winds - 11
sometimes a mountain... - 58
songs of you - 12
stitched up carelessly - 21
the lovers - 18
the sea - 40
the valley - 22
there grew around me - 56
three years in may - 47
to be loved - 42
twisted shadows - 15
you always slip through my fingers - 44
will i ever leave this dead end town - 50

a requiem of remembrance index

3:42 am - 69
a book of you - 94
a light to cut through the darkness? - 74
abandoned houses - 65
about the letter you found... - 73
all the times you prayed - 96
be of good heart - 64
brick & mortar - 98
catharsis - 81
endless waiting - 89
exhaustion - 95
fall - 105
family values - 77
holiday hell part I - 78
holiday hell part II - 79
i am - 100
i am my own worst enemy - 66
i exist too much - 99
i hate this part of texas / the tavern - 101
i know nothing about you - 80
i never lost it - 62

i want love, not apologies - 90
i want to be a feeling - 72
january 2018 - 87
like my mother - 70
love is always pain - 86
mirror image - 92
monsters under my bed - 83
never be the same - 68
paralyzed - 67
peace in solitude - 88
persephone - 102
please find your way back - 82
spring - 107
summer - 104
the days of our youth - 91
the hum - 71
the fall he returned - 85
the ocean has always... - 97
the summer he left - 84
the weight of the unknown - 63
through the seasons - 93
winter - 106

about the author

keiran james is the self published author of the book ephemerality. she spends her days lost in daydreams of far away places and fictional worlds. occasionally uploads videos on youtube (whenever she remembers to anyway). keiran is currently working on her third (and fourth) poetry collection.

instagram is @keiranonfilm

business email is keiranonfilm@gmail.com

Made in the USA
Coppell, TX
21 February 2022